J   Storey, Rita
750
STO   Painting and drawing

11/9 ⊘

I Love Crafts

Painting
and
Drawing

Rita Storey

PowerKiDS press

Published in 2017 by
The Rosen Publishing Group, Inc.
29 East 21st Street, New York, NY 10010

CATALOGING-IN-PUBLICATION DATA
Names: Storey, Rita.
Title: Painting and drawing / Rita Storey.
Description: New York : PowerKids Press, 2017. | Series: I love crafts | Includes index.
Identifiers: ISBN 9781508150725 (pbk.) | ISBN 9781508150664 (library bound) |
ISBN 9781508150558 (6 pack)
Subjects: LCSH: Painting--Juvenile literature. | Drawing--Juvenile literature. |
Handicraft--Juvenile literature.
Classification: LCC ND1146.S76 2017 | DDC 750--dc23

Designer: Rita Storey
Editor: Sarah Ridley
Crafts made by: Rita Storey
Series editor: Sarah Peutrill
Photography: Tudor Photography, Banbury
Cover images: Tudor Photography, Banbury

Manufactured in the United States of America
CPSIA Compliance Information: Batch #BS16PK:
For Further Information contact Rosen Publishing, New York, New York at 1-800-237-9932

Before you start

Some of the projects in this book require
scissors, glue, a microwave oven, acrylic paint
and sharp objects. When using these things
we would recommend that children are
supervised by a responsible adult.

Please note: Keep homemade products
away from babies and small children.
They cannot be tested for safety.

A Note About Measurements

Measurements are given in U.S.
format with metric in parentheses.
The metric conversion is rounded
to make it easier to measure.

Contents

Doodle Bookmark

Doodles are random shapes and patterns. People sometimes make designs called "doodles" when they are on the telephone or thinking about something else.

You will need:

* fine point felt-tip pens: black, green, red

* Two pieces of thin white card stock, 2 inch by 8 inch (5cm × 20cm)

* 4 inch (10cm) length of thin ribbon

* white glue and spreader

You can use colored ballpoint pens instead of felt-tip pens.

1 Using the black felt-tip pen, doodle some shapes on one piece of card stock. Copy the pattern shown above or make up your own.

2 Draw smaller shapes inside each large shape.

3 Fill in the spaces between each shape with lines or patterns, as shown.

4 Use the black felt-tip pen to make some of the lines thicker.

5 Draw patterns between some of the lines using the red felt-tip pen.

6 Use the green felt-tip pen to fill in more areas and complete the design. Repeat steps 1–6 to decorate the other piece of card stock.

7 Lay one of the pieces of card stock with the decorated side facedown. Spread the card stock with glue. Fold the ribbon in half and place the doubled over ends at one end. Spread some more glue over the ribbon as shown.

8 Press the undecorated side of the second piece of card stock onto the glue with the ribbon sandwiched in between. Leave to dry.

Leave the bookmark between the pages of a book to mark your place.

Frog Flip Book

Flip the pages and watch this hungry frog catch his lunch!

You will need:

* a small pad of sticky notes (or staple some squares of colored paper together)

* black felt-tip pen

You could hold the paper up to a bright window to help you trace the picture.

1 Use the felt-tip pen to draw a frog on the lower half of the last sticky note in the pad. Copy the frog on page 32 or make up your own.

2 Working from the back, flip down the next sticky note. Trace the frog through the paper, onto this sticky note. Draw a fly to the left of the frog.

3 Repeat step 2 and add the tip of the frog's tongue, sticking out of its mouth.

4 Repeat step 2 several times. Every time you draw the frog, show its tongue getting longer and closer to the fly.

5 Draw the frog's tongue touching the fly.

6 In the next picture, draw the frog's mouth closed and leave the fly out of the picture.

7 Draw a few more pictures with the corners of the frog's mouth curling up into a smile.

8 Take hold of the pad with your fingers on the top and your thumb at the bottom. Lift the pages up.

9 Let the pages go, one at a time, so that you flick through the sticky notes from the back of the pad to the front.

10 As you let the sticky notes go, the picture will appear to move.

These pictures show six stages. The more stages you put into a flip book the better. In your flip book, make the tongue only a tiny bit bigger each time.

Fabric Wall Hanging

Paint a design with white glue onto a piece of fabric to create a unique wall hanging for your bedroom.

You will need:

* 1 piece of white cotton fabric, 6 inch by 15½ inch (15cm × 40cm)
* white glue with a pouring nozzle
* white glue and spreader
* yellow acrylic paint
* water * small paint pots or jars
* paintbrush
* green acrylic paint
* baking sheet
* warm, soapy water
* paper towel
* two straight sticks, 1½ inches (4cm) longer than the width of the fabric
* ruler
* 15½-inch (40cm) length of string

To make this wall hanging you will need space to leave the fabric to dry for up to two days. Before you begin, check that the space is not needed for anything else.

1 Using the white glue with the pouring nozzle, dribble glue onto the fabric in the shape of leaves. Add some decorative patterns. Leave the glue to dry.

2 Mix a squeeze of the yellow acrylic paint with the same amount of water in a small paint pot. Paint over some areas of the fabric and dried glue, as shown. Leave it to dry.

3 Mix a squeeze of the green acrylic paint with the same amount of water in another small paint pot. Paint over different areas of the fabric. Leave it to dry.

4 Soak the fabric in warm, soapy water in the baking sheet for 15 minutes. Carefully place the wet fabric onto a layer of paper towel. Peel off the glue. Leave the fabric to dry.

5 Place the fabric paint-side down. Spread glue along the edge of the top of the fabric. Fold the top ¾ inch (2cm) over and press it down.

6 Repeat step 5 along the bottom edge of the fabric. Leave it to dry. Slide the sticks through the gaps you have created, top and bottom. Knot the string onto the top stick on either side of the wall hanging so that you can hang it up.

Snake Box

The snake design on this box is inspired by Aboriginal paintings. Use the box to keep your precious possessions safe.

You will need:

* flat cardboard box
* blue paint
* paintbrushes
* thin white paper and pencil (for tracing the template)
* scissors
* fine point black felt-tip pen
* dark purple paint
* paper towel
* white paint
* yellow paint
* 2 stick-on jewels

If you like this style of painting, use library books or the Internet to research Aborigine paintings.

1 Paint the box blue all over. Leave it to dry.

2 Use thin white paper and a pencil to trace the snake template on page 31. Cut it out.

3 Draw around the snake template on the box's lid with the black felt-tip pen. Remove the template.

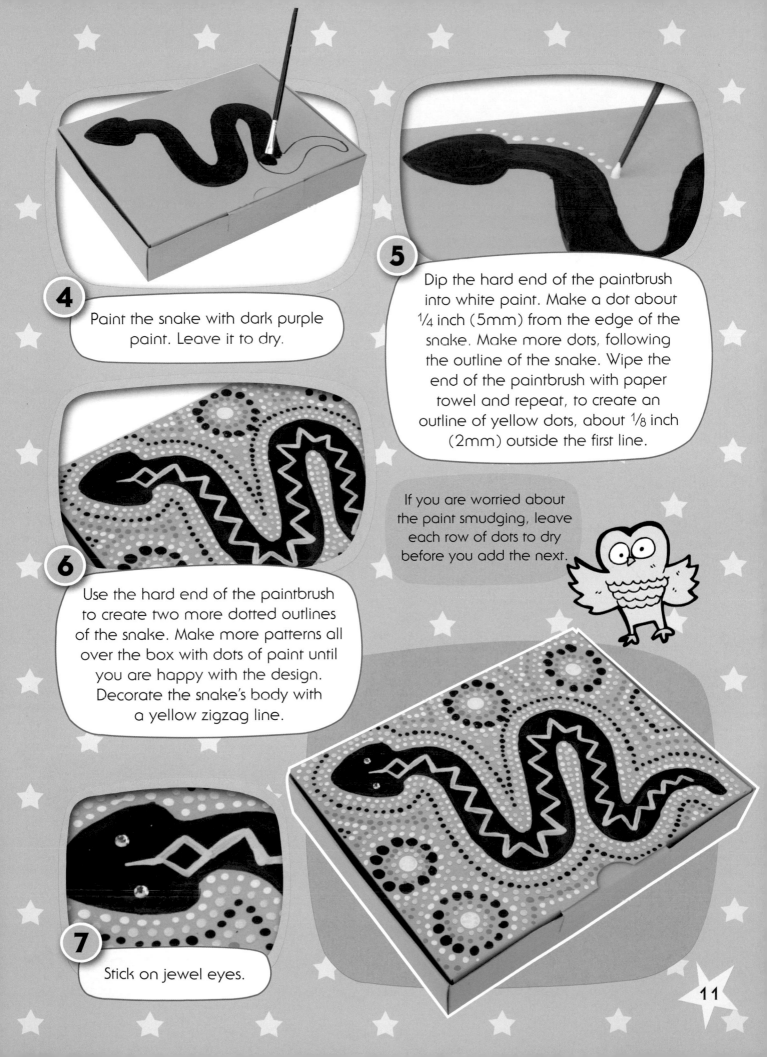

4 Paint the snake with dark purple paint. Leave it to dry.

5 Dip the hard end of the paintbrush into white paint. Make a dot about ¼ inch (5mm) from the edge of the snake. Make more dots, following the outline of the snake. Wipe the end of the paintbrush with paper towel and repeat, to create an outline of yellow dots, about ⅛ inch (2mm) outside the first line.

If you are worried about the paint smudging, leave each row of dots to dry before you add the next.

6 Use the hard end of the paintbrush to create two more dotted outlines of the snake. Make more patterns all over the box with dots of paint until you are happy with the design. Decorate the snake's body with a yellow zigzag line.

7 Stick on jewel eyes.

Puffy Paint Picture

This paint works like magic. Watch your painting puff up in the microwave to create a great 3-D effect.

You will need:

* mixing bowl
* 6 tablespoons of self-rising flour
* 6 tablespoons of salt
* water
* three small mixing bowls or dishes
* brown ink or food coloring
* yellow ink or food coloring
* green ink or food coloring
* empty squeeze bottles (small soap bottles or empty paint bottles)
* sheet of thick green paper or thin green card stock, 7 inch by 7 inch (18cm × 18cm)
* microwave oven

1 Measure the self-rising flour into the mixing bowl. Add the salt. Mix with water to make a smooth paste.

2 Divide the mixture into three small mixing bowls. Mix brown ink or food coloring into one bowl, yellow into another and green into the last one.

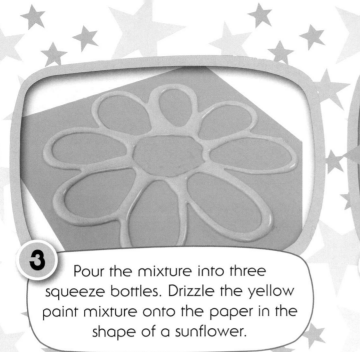

3 Pour the mixture into three squeeze bottles. Drizzle the yellow paint mixture onto the paper in the shape of a sunflower.

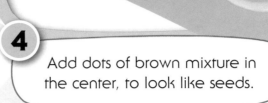

4 Add dots of brown mixture in the center, to look like seeds.

5 Drizzle green mixture to make a stem and leaves to finish.

6 Ask an adult to microwave the picture for 30 seconds. The paint will puff up and harden.

Op Art Butterfly

This type of picture is based on geometric shapes. It has a real wow factor.

You will need:

* thin white paper and pencil (to trace the template)
* scissors
* fine point black felt-tip pen
* square of white card stock, 8 inch by 8 inch (20cm × 20cm)
* ruler   * glue and spreader
* green, blue, and purple felt-tip pens
* yellow, orange, and red felt-tip pens
* thick black card stock, 10 inch by 10 inch (25cm × 25cm)

Op art stands for optical art, a style of painting made famous by artists such as Bridget Riley.

1 Use thin white paper and a pencil to trace the butterfly template on page 31. Cut it out. Use the black felt-tip pen to draw around it on the white card stock.

2 Using a ruler, draw lines in black felt-tip pen from the top to the bottom of the card stock. Angle some lines and vary the distance between them.

14

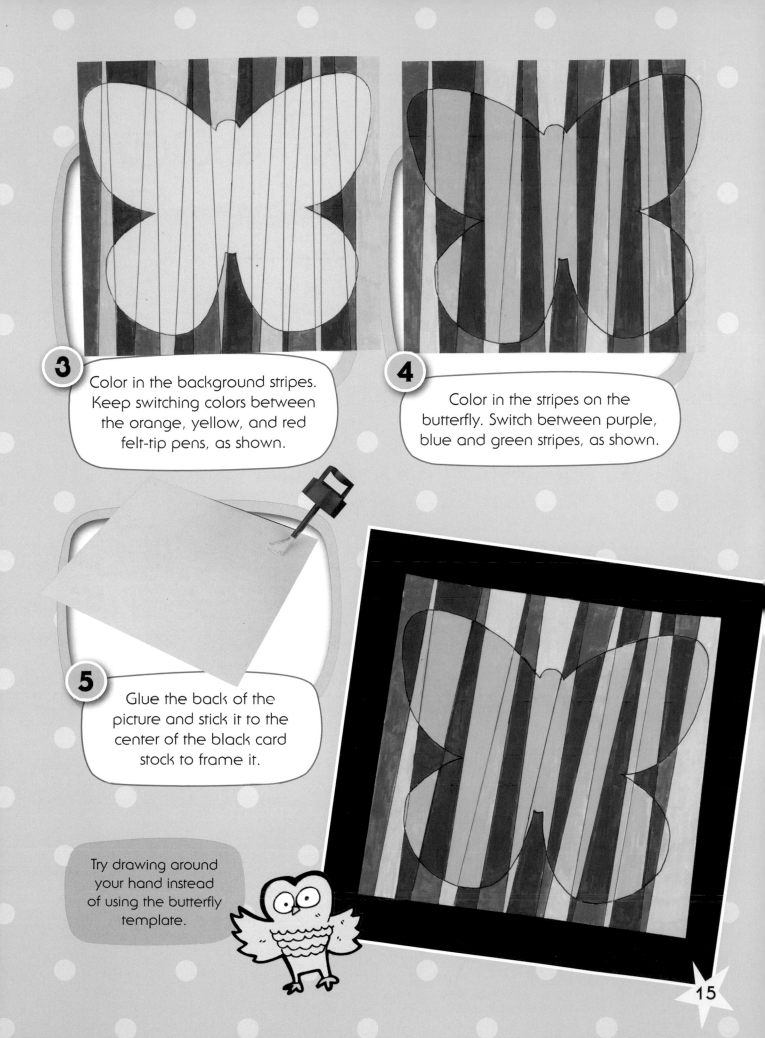

3 Color in the background stripes. Keep switching colors between the orange, yellow, and red felt-tip pens, as shown.

4 Color in the stripes on the butterfly. Switch between purple, blue and green stripes, as shown.

5 Glue the back of the picture and stick it to the center of the black card stock to frame it.

Try drawing around your hand instead of using the butterfly template.

15

Underwater Scene

Salt sprinkled on wet watercolor paint makes interesting patterns and textures – just right for an underwater scene.

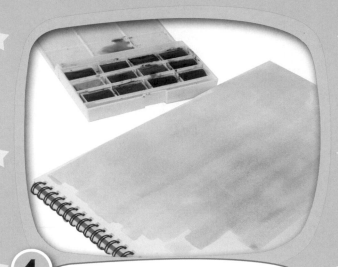

You will need:

* watercolor paper
* blue and green watercolors
* paint palette
* paintbrush
* water
* salt
* magazines
* scissors
* feathers
* glue and spreader
* a party popper

1 Mix blue and green watercolor paint with water in a paint palette. Paint the watercolor paper blue and green.

You can make your own watercolor paper by following the instructions on page 30.

2 Sprinkle salt onto the wet paint and leave everything to dry.

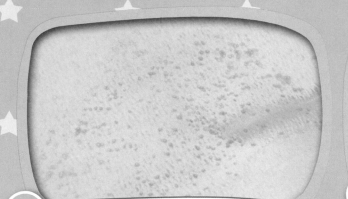

3 Brush off the salt, to leave interesting patterns in the paint.

4 Cut fish shapes from magazines. Choose interesting patterns or colors. Glue the fish onto the picture.

5 Glue the feathers onto the bottom of the picture as seaweed.

Cut an uneven strip of paper from a magazine. Glue it along the bottom of the picture to look like the seabed. **6**

7 Pop the party popper, remembering to point it away from people. Glue on some of the party popper strings to look like strands of seaweed.

Abstract Notepad

Make a plain notepad cover into a real work of art. This abstract style of painting was used by a famous painter called Mondrian.

You will need:

* ballpoint pen
* notepad
* sheet of black card stock
* scissors
* masking tape
* paintbrush
* white acrylic paint
* yellow acrylic paint
* red acrylic paint
* double-sided adhesive tape

1 Use the pen to draw around the bottom and sides of the notepad cover onto the black card stock. Join up the lines as shown in blue. Cut out the shape.

Masking tape is easy to peel off the surface of the cover. Do not use adhesive tape as it will tear the cover when you peel it off.

2 Tape strips of masking tape in horizontal and vertical lines onto the black card stock, as shown.

3 Painting over the masking tape, paint some of the areas of card stock in white, some in yellow and the rest in red. Leave to dry.

4 Carefully peel off the masking tape.

5 Fix double-sided adhesive tape along each edge on the back of the card stock.

6 Remove the backing tape to fix the new notepad cover in place.
You can use this technique to decorate storage boxes and folders too.

Pop Art Poster

Print a simple self-portrait onto colorful paper squares and join them together to make a dramatic poster for your room.

You will need:

* flat Styrofoam, 4 inch by 4 inch (10cm × 10cm)

* ballpoint pen

* scrap paper

* paintbrush

* white paint * black paint

* 4 squares of orange paper, 4 inch by 4 inch (10cm × 10cm)

* 4 squares of pink paper, 4 inch by 4 inch (10cm × 10cm)

* 4 squares of green paper, 4 inch by 4 inch (10cm × 10cm)

* paper towel

* masking tape

* sheet of stiff black paper, 13½ inch by 17½ inch (34cm × 44cm)

* White glue and spreader

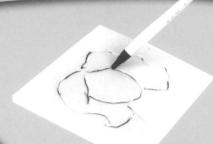

1 Draw a simple self-portrait onto the Styrofoam using a ballpoint pen. Press hard so that the lines are deep.

2 Paint a layer of white paint onto the Styrofoam. Press it down onto scrap paper to get rid of any excess paint.

3 Press the foam printing block onto one of the orange paper squares. Lift it off and leave the print to dry.

4 Use the foam block to print onto one more orange, two pink and two green squares of paper.

5 Wash the white paint off the foam block under a running tap. Dry the Styrofoam with paper towel. Paint the printing block with black paint. Use it to print onto two pink, two green and two orange squares of paper.

6 Leave to dry. Arrange the prints in a pattern, mixing up the colors and the black and white prints. Turn all the printed pictures face down.

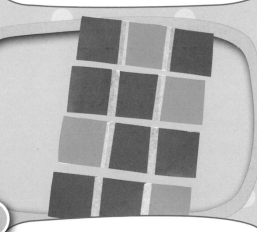

7 Use masking tape to join all the squares into rows, as shown. Tape all the rows together. Glue everything onto black paper to finish your poster.

Bubble Painting

Have fun creating beautiful printed patterns with a bowl full of bubbles. Work quickly before the bubbles burst.

1 Put two teaspoons of orange food coloring into a small bowl.

You will need:

* orange, purple and blue food coloring or ink
* teaspoon
* small bowl
* dishwashing liquid * water
* plastic drinking straw
* letter-sized white paper
* letter-sized white card stock

2 Add two teaspoons of dishwashing liquid. Add four teaspoons of water. Mix everything together with the spoon.

If you are using ink, be very careful not to suck on the straw and swallow it.

3 Use the straw to blow into the colored liquid to make lots of bubbles.

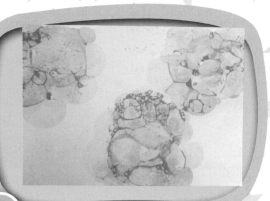

4 Gently place a sheet of paper on top of the bubbles. Take a print of the orange bubbles.

5 Move the paper over, to take two more prints from the bubbles. Leave the paint to dry.

6 Repeat steps 1–3, using a clean bowl and blue food coloring. Place the sheet of paper with the orange bubble prints on top of the blue bubbles. Repeat steps 4–5. Leave to dry.

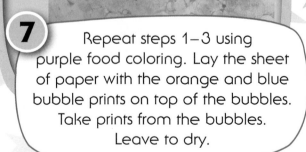

7 Repeat steps 1–3 using purple food coloring. Lay the sheet of paper with the orange and blue bubble prints on top of the bubbles. Take prints from the bubbles. Leave to dry.

8 You could repeat steps 1–7 using thin card stock. Fold the card in half and use it as a birthday card.

23

Heart Bunting

Practice some of the techniques used in this book and make a great room decoration at the same time.

Use thin white paper and a pencil to trace the heart template on page 31. Cut it out.

Watercolor Hearts

You will need:

* pencil and thin white paper (for tracing the template)

* scissors

* letter-sized card stock

* string

* small pegs

AND

For the watercolor hearts:

* watercolor paints (blue, green, pink, and purple)

* paintbrush

* water

* fine point felt-tip pen

For the dotted hearts:

* poster paints (blue, white, yellow, and red)

* paintbrush

* felt-tip pen

1 Take one sheet of white card stock and paint some parts with blue watercolor paint and others with green watercolor paint. Wash the brush in clean water.

2 Blend the colors together using a clean wet paintbrush. Leave to dry.

3 Use the black felt-tip pen to draw around the heart template, as shown. Cut it out.

4 Repeat steps 1–3 using a fresh piece of white card stock and pink and purple watercolors to make a second heart.

Dotted Hearts

1 Use the template to cut a heart shape from white card stock. Paint it with blue poster paint and leave it to dry.

2 Dip the end of a felt-tip pen in white poster paint. Press it onto the heart. Repeat to make a line of dots that follows the outline of the heart.

3 Dip the end of a paintbrush in yellow paint to make a second line inside the first. You could complete your design by repeating the dotted heart shapes in the center, as shown below. Make another heart with a yellow painted background.

This heart is cut out of bubble print paper. The instructions for this are on pages 22–23.

Peg the hearts onto the string. Tie the loose ends of the string to hang up the bunting.

Fireworks

The fireworks in this picture burst through the black paint as you scrape off the surface.

You will need:

* pink, green, red and yellow wax crayons

* newspaper

* black poster paint

* paintbrush

* sheet of letter-sized thick white paper

* sheet of letter-sized thin white paper

* colored pencil

* paper clip, opened out

1 Use the wax crayons to color thick stripes of wax over an entire sheet of paper. Do not leave any bits of paper showing through.

Try scratching off the paint with a lollipop stick or a toothpick to get different effects.

2 Put the sheet of paper onto a layer of newspaper. Use poster paint to paint the paper black. Leave to dry. If the wax crayon is showing through, add a second layer of paint.

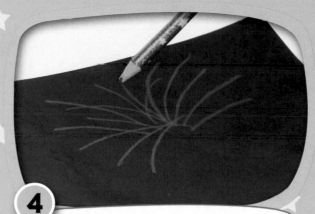

3 Sketch some exploding fireworks on the piece of thin white paper.

4 Copy the design onto the black paint with the colored pencil.

5 Use the end of the opened out paper clip to scratch off the black paint, following the pencil lines. This will reveal the wax crayon colors underneath.

Try drawing thick circles of wax instead of stripes for a different effect.

Totem Pole

The rich bright colors of felt-tip pens make this totem pole very eye-catching.

You will need:

* cardboard tube from inside a paper towel roll

* piece of white paper the same height as the tube and wide enough to wrap around it with an overlap of 3/8 inch (1cm)

* pencil

* ruler

* fine point black felt-tip pen

* colored felt-tip pens

* double-sided adhesive tape

* scissors

A totem pole is a tree or carved wooden pole decorated with animals or symbols.

1 Use a pencil to draw a bird's eyes and a beak in the center of the paper, 3/4 inch (2cm) from the top. Draw a second set of eyes and a beak 2¾ inches (7cm) from the bottom. Draw feet above the bottom set of eyes. Draw feathers over the rest of the paper, as shown below.

2 Go over the pencil lines with the black felt-tip pen.

3 Use felt-tip pens to color in the designs.

4 Turn the paper over. Put a strip of double-sided tape down each side of the design. Peel the backing strip off one piece of tape and lay the tube onto it.

5 Peel the backing strip off the second piece of tape. Wrap your picture around the tube. Press it in place.

6 Use the template on page 32 to trace two pairs of wings. Cut them out.

7 Copy the wing design shown above or create one of your own. Go over the lines with black felt-tip pen. Use the felt-tip pens to color in the pattern. Use a short strip of double-sided tape to fix the wings to the back of the totem pole, as shown in the finished picture on the right.

Watercolor Paper

Make your own watercolor paper and use it to paint like a real watercolor artist. To make your own watercolor paper you wet paper that is taped to a board. It will wrinkle at first but once it has dried it will not wrinkle again when you paint on it.

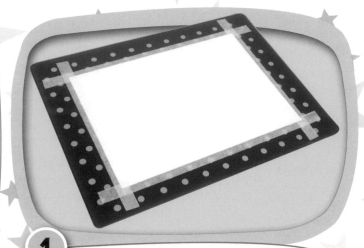

1 Tape all the sides of the paper to the cutting board, as shown, and press it down firmly with your fingers.

You will need:

* masking tape
* letter-sized, sturdy, smooth paper
* clean chopping or cutting board
* paintbrush
* water

2 Use the paintbrush to brush a layer of water over the paper. It will wrinkle. Leave it to dry – it will flatten as it dries. Carefully remove the masking tape. Now you have a sheet of watercolor paper.

Templates

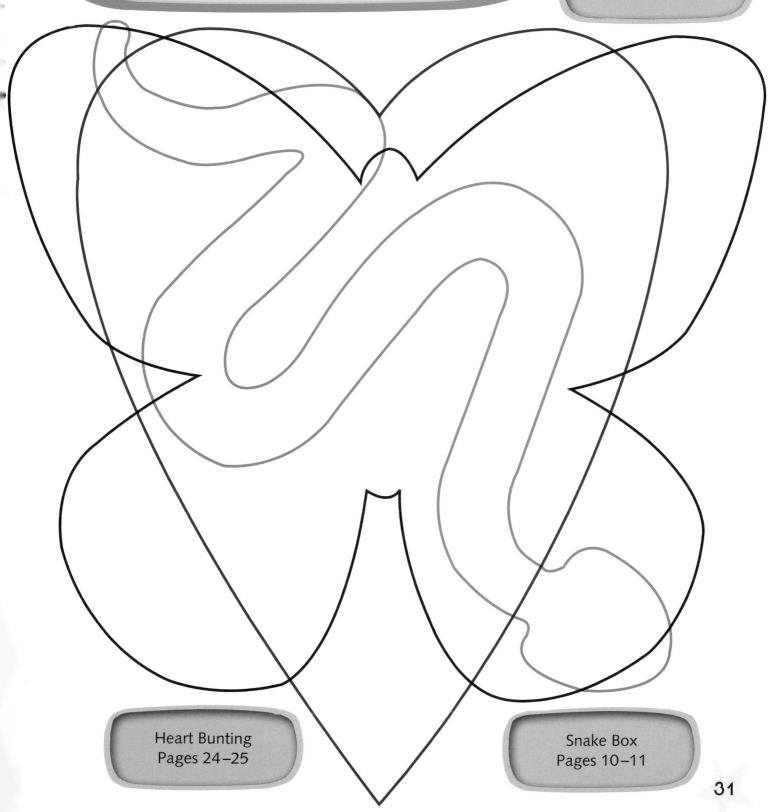

Frog Flip Book
Pages 6–7

Totem Pole
Pages 28–29

Index

Further Information

Books

Art Treasury by Rosie Dickins (Usborne, 2007)
An introduction to famous artists and artworks with simple projects based on the techniques they used.

Websites

PowerKids Press has developed an online list of websites related to the subject of this book. This site is updated regularly. Please use this link to access the list:
www.powerkidslinks.com/ilc/paint